Coriolanus

Plutarch

TRANSLATED BY

JOHN DRYDEN

ANOTHER LEAF PRESS

```
     *
    ***
   ******
    ***
     *


     *
    ***
   *******
  **********
   ******
    ***
     *


     *
    ***
   ******
    ***
     *
```

ANOTHER LEAF PRESS

2013

Coriolanus

The patrician house of the Marcii in Rome produced many men of distinction, and among the rest, Ancus Marcius, grandson to Numa by his daughter, and king after Tullus Hostilius. Of the same family were also Publius and Quintus Marcius, which two conveyed into the city the best and most abundant supply of water they have at Rome. As likewise Censorinus, who, having been twice chosen censor by the people, afterwards himself induced them to make a law that nobody should bear that office twice. But Caius Marcius, of whom I now write, being left an orphan, and brought up under the widowhood of his mother, has shown us by experience, that, although the early loss of a father may be attended with other disadvantages, yet it can hinder none from being either virtuous or eminent in the world, and that it is no obstacle to true goodness and excellence; however bad men may be pleased to lay the blame of their corruptions upon that misfortune and the neglect of them in their minority. Nor is he less an evidence to the truth of their opinion, who conceive that a generous and worthy nature without proper discipline, like a rich soil without culture, is apt, with its better fruits, to produce also much that is bad and faulty. While the force and vigor of his soul, and a persevering constancy in all he undertook, led him successfully into many noble achievements, yet, on the other side, also, by indulging the vehemence of his passion, and through all obstinate reluctance to yield or accommodate his humors and sentiments to those of people about him, he rendered himself incapable of acting and associating with others. Those who saw with admiration how proof his nature was against all the softnesses of pleasure, the hardships of service, and the allurements of gain, while allowing to that universal firmness of his the respective names of temperance, fortitude, and justice, yet, in the life of the citizen and the statesman, could not choose but be disgusted at the severity and ruggedness of his deportment, and with his overbearing, haughty, and imperious temper. Education and study, and the favors of the muses, confer no greater benefit on those that seek them, than these humanizing and civilizing lessons, which teach our natural qualities to submit to the limitations prescribed by reason, and to avoid the wildness of extremes.

Those were times at Rome in which that kind of worth was most esteemed which displayed itself in military achievements; one evidence of which we find in the Latin word for virtue, which is properly equivalent to manly courage. As if valor and all virtue had been the same thing, they used as the common term the name of the particular excellence. But Marcius, having a more passionate inclination than any of that age for feats of war, began at once, from his very childhood, to handle arms; and feeling that adventitious implements and artificial arms would effect little, and be of small use to such as have not their native and natural weapons well fixed and prepared for service, he so exercised and inured his body to all sorts of activity and encounter, that, besides the lightness of a racer, he had a weight in close seizures and wrestlings with an enemy, from which it was hard for any to disengage himself; so that his competitors at home in displays of bravery, loath to own themselves inferior in that respect, were wont to ascribe their deficiencies to his strength of body, which they said no resistance and no fatigue could exhaust.

The first time he went out to the wars, being yet a stripling, was when Tarquinius Superbus, who had been king of Rome and was afterwards expelled, after many unsuccessful attempts, now entered upon his last effort, and proceeded to hazard all as it were upon a single throw. A great number of the Latins and other people of Italy joined their forces, and were marching with him toward the city, to procure his restoration; not, however, so much out of a desire to serve and oblige Tarquin, as to gratify their own fear and envy at the increase of the Roman greatness, which they were anxious to check and reduce. The armies met and engaged in a decisive battle, in the vicissitudes of which, Marcius, while fighting bravely in the dictator's presence, saw a Roman soldier struck down at a little distance, and immediately stepped in and stood before him, and slew his assailant. The general, after having gained the victory, crowned him for this act, one of the first, with a garland of oaken branches; it being the Roman custom thus to adorn those who had saved the life of a citizen; whether that the law intended some special honor to the oak, in memory of the Arcadians, a people the oracle had made famous by the name of acorn-eaters; or whether the reason of it was because they might easily, and in all places where they fought, have plenty of oak for that purpose; or, finally, whether the oaken wreath, being sacred to Jupiter, the guardian of the city, might, therefore, be thought a propel ornament for one who preserved a citizen. And the oak, in truth, is the tree which bears the most and the prettiest fruit of any that grow wild, and is the strongest of all that are under cultivation; its acorns were the principal diet of the first mortals, and the honey found in it gave them drink. I may say, too, it furnished fowl and other creatures as dainties, in producing mistletoe for birdlime to ensnare them. In this battle, meantime, it is stated that Castor and Pollux appeared, and, immediately after the battle, were seen at Rome just by the fountain where their temple now stands, with their horses foaming with sweat, and told the news of the victory to the people in the Forum. The fifteenth of July, being the day of this conquest, became consequently a solemn holiday sacred to the Twin Brothers.

It may be observed in general, that when young men arrive early at fame and repute, if they are of a nature but slightly touched with emulation, this early attainment is apt to extinguish their thirst and satiate their small appetite; whereas the first distinctions of more solid and weighty characters do but stimulate and quicken them and take them away, like a wind, in the pursuit of honor; they look upon these marks and testimonies to their virtue not as a recompense received for what they have already done, but as a pledge given by themselves of what they will perform hereafter, ashamed now to forsake or underlive the credit they have won, or, rather, not to exceed and obscure all that is gone before by the luster of their following actions. Marcius, having a spirit of this noble make, was ambitious always to surpass himself, and did nothing, how extraordinary soever, but he thought he was bound to outdo it at the next occasion; and ever desiring to give continual fresh instances of his prowess he added one exploit to another, and heaped up trophies upon trophies, so as to make it a matter of contest also among his commanders, the later still vying with the earlier, which should pay him the greatest honor and speak highest in his commendation. Of all the numerous wars and conflicts in those days, there was not one from which he returned without laurels and rewards.

And, whereas others made glory the end of their daring, the end of his glory was his mother's gladness; the delight she took to hear him praised and to see him crowned, and her weeping for joy in his embraces, rendered him, in his own thoughts, the most honored and most happy person in the world. Epaminondas is similarly said to have acknowledged his feeling, that it was the greatest felicity of his whole life that his father and mother survived to hear of his successful generalship and his victory at Leuctra. And he had the advantage, indeed, to have both his parents partake with him, and enjoy the pleasure of his good fortune. But Marcius, believing himself bound to pay his mother Volumnia all that gratitude and duty which would have belonged to his father, had he also been alive, could never satiate himself in his tenderness and respect to her. He took a wife, also, at her request and wish, and continued, even after he had children, to live still with his mother, without parting families.

The repute of his integrity and courage had, by this time, gained him a considerable influence and authority in Rome, when the senate, favoring the wealthier citizens, began to be at variance with the common people, who made sad complaints of the rigorous and inhuman usage they received from the money-lenders. For as many as were behind with them, and had any sort of property, they stripped of all they had, by the way of pledges and sales; and such as through former exactions were reduced already to extreme indigence, and had nothing more to be deprived of, these they led away in person and put their bodies under constraint, notwithstanding the scars and wounds that they could show in attestation of their public services in numerous campaigns; the last of which had been against the Sabines, which they undertook upon a promise made by their rich creditors that they would treat them with more gentleness for the future, Marcus Valerius, the consul, having, by order from the senate, engaged also for the performance of it. But when, after they had fought courageously and beaten the enemy, there was, nevertheless, no moderation or forbearance used, and the senate also professed to remember nothing of that agreement, and sat without testifying the least concern to see them dragged away like slaves and their goods seized upon as formerly, there began now to be open disorders and dangerous meetings in the city; and the enemy, also, aware of the popular confusion, invaded and laid waste the country. And when the consuls now gave notice, that all who were of an age to bear arms should make their personal appearance, but found no one regard the summons, the members of the government, then coming to consult what course should be taken, were themselves again divided in opinion: some thought it most advisable to comply a little in favor of the poor, by relaxing their overstrained rights, and mitigating the extreme rigor of the law, while others withstood this proposal; Marcius in particular, with more vehemence than the rest, alleging that the business of money on either side was not the main thing in question, urged that this disorderly proceeding was but the first insolent step towards open revolt against the laws, which it would become the wisdom of the government to check at the earliest moment.

There had been frequent assemblies of the whole senate, within a small compass of time, about this difficulty, but without any certain issue; the poor commonalty, therefore, perceiving there was likely to be no redress of their grievances, on a sudden collected in a body, and, encouraging each other in their resolution, forsook the city with one accord and seizing the hill which is now called the Holy Mount, sat down by the river Anio, without committing any sort of violence or seditious outrage, but merely exclaiming, as they went along, that they had this long time past been, in fact, expelled and excluded from the city by the cruelty of the rich; that Italy would everywhere afford them the benefit of air and water and a place of burial, which was all they could expect in the city, unless it were, perhaps, the privilege of being wounded and killed in time of war for the defense of their creditors. The senate, apprehending the consequences, sent the most moderate and popular men of their own order to treat with them.

Menenius Agrippa, their chief spokesman, after much entreaty to the people, and much plain speaking on behalf of the senate, concluded, at length, with the celebrated fable. "It once happened," he said, "that all the other members of a man mutinied against the stomach, which they accused as the only idle, uncontributing part in the whole body, while the rest were put to hardships and the expense of much labor to supply and minister to its appetites. The stomach, however, merely ridiculed the silliness of the members, who appeared not to be aware that the stomach certainly does receive the general nourishment, but only to return it again, and redistribute it amongst the rest. Such is the case," he said, "ye citizens, between you and the senate. The counsels and plans that are there duly digested, convey and secure to all of you, your proper benefit and support."

A reconciliation ensued, the senate acceding to the request of the people for the annual election of five protectors for those in need of succor, the same that are now called the tribunes of the people; and the first two they pitched upon were Junius Brutus and Sicinnius Vellutus, their leaders in the secession.

The city being thus united, the commons stood presently to their arms, and followed their commanders to the war with great alacrity. As for Marcius, though he was not a little vexed himself to see the populace prevail so far and gain ground of the senators, and might observe many other patricians have the same dislike of the late concessions, he yet besought them not to yield at least to the common people in the zeal and forwardness they now allowed for their country's service, but to prove that they were superior to them, not so much in power and riches as in merit and worth.

The Romans were now at war with the Volscian nation, whose principal city was Corioli; when, therefore, Cominius the consul had invested this important place, the rest of the Volscians, fearing it would be taken, mustered up whatever force they could from all parts, to relieve it, designing to give the Romans battle before the city, and so attack them on both sides. Cominius, to avoid this inconvenience, divided his army, marching himself with one body to encounter the Volscians on their approach from without, and leaving Titus Lartius, one of the bravest Romans of his time, to command the other and continue the siege. Those within Corioli, despising now the smallness of their number, made a sally upon them, and prevailed at first, and pursued the Romans into their trenches. Here it was that Marcius, flying out with a slender company, and cutting those in pieces that first engaged him, obliged the other assailants to slacken their speed; and then, with loud cries, called upon the Romans to renew the battle. For he had, what Cato thought a great point in a soldier, not only strength of hand and stroke, but also a voice and look that of themselves were a terror to an enemy. Divers of his own party now rallying and making up to him, the enemies soon retreated; but Marcius, not content to see them draw off and retire, pressed hard upon the rear, and drove them, as they fled away in haste, to the very gates of their city; where, perceiving the Romans to fall back from their pursuit, beaten off by the multitude of darts poured in upon them from the walls, and that none of his followers had the hardiness to think of falling in pellmell among the fugitives and so entering a city full of enemies in arms, he, nevertheless, stood and urged them to the attempt, crying out, that fortune had now set open Corioli, not so much to shelter the vanquished, as to receive the conquerors. Seconded by a few that were willing to venture with him, he bore along through the crowd, made good his passage, and thrust himself into the gate through the midst of them, nobody at first daring to resist him. But when the citizens, on looking about, saw that a very small number had entered, they now took courage, and came up and attacked them. A combat ensued of the most extraordinary description, in which Marcius, by strength of hand, and swiftness of foot, and daring of soul, overpowering every one that he assailed, succeeded in driving the enemy to seek refuge, for the most part, in the interior of the town, while the remainder submitted, and threw down their arms; thus affording Lartius abundant opportunity to bring in the rest of the Romans with ease and safety.

Corioli being thus surprised and taken, the greater part of the soldiers employed themselves in spoiling and pillaging it, while Marcius indignantly reproached them, and exclaimed that it was a dishonorable and unworthy thing, when the consul and their fellow-citizens had now perhaps encountered the other Volscians, and were hazarding their lives in battle, basely to misspend the time in running up and down for booty, and, under a pretense of enriching themselves, keep out of danger. Few paid him any attention, but, putting himself at the head of these, he took the road by which the consul's army had marched before him, encouraging his companions, and beseeching them, as they went along, not to give up, and praying often to the gods, too, that he might be so happy as to arrive before the fight was over, and come seasonably up to assist Cominius, and partake in the peril of the action.

It was customary with the Romans of that age, when they were moving into battle array, and were on the point of taking up their bucklers, and girding their coats about them, to make at the same time an unwritten will, or verbal testament, and to name who should be their heirs, in the hearing of three or four witnesses. In this precise posture Marcius found them at his arrival, the enemy being advanced within view.

They were not a little disturbed by his first appearance, seeing him covered with blood and sweat, and attended with a small train; but when he hastily made up to the consul with gladness in his looks, giving him his hand, and recounting to him how the city had been taken, and when they saw Cominius also embrace and salute him, every one took fresh heart; those that were near enough hearing, and those that were at a distance guessing, what had happened; and all cried out to be led to battle. First, however, Marcius desired to know of him how the Volscians had arrayed their army, and where they had placed their best men, and on his answering that he took the troops of the Antiates in the center to be their prime warriors, that would yield to none in bravery, "Let me then demand and obtain of you," said Marcius, "that we may be posted against them." The consul granted the request, with much admiration of his gallantry. And when the conflict began by the soldiers darting at each other, and Marcius sallied out before the rest, the Volscians opposed to him were not able to make head against him; wherever he fell in, he broke their ranks, and made a lane through them; but the parties turning again, and enclosing him on each side with their weapons, the consul, who observed the danger he was in, dispatched some of the choicest men he had for his rescue. The conflict then growing warm and sharp about Marcius, and many falling dead in a little space, the Romans bore so hard upon the enemies, and pressed them with such violence, that they forced them at length to abandon their ground, and to quit the field. And, going now to prosecute the victory, they besought Marcius, tired out with his toils, and faint and heavy through the loss of blood, that he would retire to the camp. He replied, however, that weariness was not for conquerors, and joined with them in the pursuit. The rest of the Volscian army was in like manner defeated, great numbers killed, and no less taken captive.

The day after, when Marcius, with the rest of the army, presented themselves at the consul's tent, Cominius rose, and having rendered all due acknowledgment to the gods for the success of that enterprise, turned next to Marcius, and first of all delivered the strongest encomium upon his rare exploits, which he had partly been an eyewitness of himself, in the late battle, and had partly learned from the testimony of Lartius. And then he required him to choose a tenth part of all the treasure and horses and captives that had fallen into their hands, before any division should be made to others; besides which, he made him the special present of a horse with trappings and ornaments, in honor of his actions. The whole army applauded; Marcius, however, stepped forth, and declaring his thankful acceptance of the horse, and his gratification at the praises of his general, said, that all other things, which he could only regard rather as mercenary advantages than any significations of honor, he must waive, and should be content with the ordinary proportion of such rewards. "I have only," said he; "one special grace to beg, and this I hope you will not deny me. There was a certain hospitable friend of mine among the Volscians, a man of probity and virtue, who is become a prisoner, and from former wealth and freedom is now reduced to servitude. Among his many misfortunes let my intercession redeem him from the one of being sold as a common slave." Such a refusal and such a request on the part of Marcius were followed with yet louder acclamations; and he had many more admirers of this generous superiority to avarice, than of the bravery he had shown in battle. The very persons who conceived some envy and despite to see him so specially honored, could not but acknowledge, that one who so nobly could refuse reward, was beyond others worthy to receive it; and were more charmed with that virtue which made him despise advantage, than with any of those former actions that had gained him his title to it. It is the hither accomplishment to use money well than to use arms; but not to need it is more noble than to use it.

When the noise of approbation and applause ceased, Cominius, resuming, said, "It is idle, fellow-soldiers, to force and obtrude those other gifts of ours on one who is unwilling to accept them ; let us, therefore, give him one of such a kind that he cannot well reject it; let us pass a vote, I mean, that he shall hereafter be called Coriolanus, unless you think that his performance at Corioli has itself anticipated any such resolution." Hence, therefore, he had his third name of Coriolanus, making it all the plainer that Caius was a personal proper name, and the second, or surname, Marcius, one common to his house and family; the third being a subsequent addition which used to be imposed either from some particular act or fortune, bodily characteristic, or good quality of the bearer. Just as the Greeks, too, gave additional names in old time, in some cases from some achievement, Soter, for example, and Callinicus; or personal appearance, as Physcon and Grypus; good qualities, Euergetes and Philadelphus; good fortune, Eudaemon, the title of the second Battus. Several monarchs have also had names given them in mockery, as Antigonus was called Doson, and Ptolemy, Lathyrus. This sort of title was yet more common among the Romans. One of the Metelli was surnamed Diadematus, because he walked about for a long time with a bandage on his head, to conceal a scar;

and another, of the same family, got the name of Celer, from the rapidity he displayed in giving a funeral entertainment of gladiators within a few days after his father's death, his speed and energy in doing which was thought extraordinary. There are some, too, who even at this day take names from certain casual incidents at their nativity; a child that is born when his father is away from home is called Proculus; or Postumus, if after his decease; and when twins come into the world, and one dies at the birth, the survivor has the name of Vopiscus. From bodily peculiarities they derive not only their Syllas and Nigers, but their Caeci and Claudii; wisely endeavoring to accustom their people not to reckon either the loss of sight, or any other bodily misfortune, as a matter of disgrace to them, but to answer to such names without shame, as if they were really their own. But this discussion better befits another place.

The war against the Volscians was no sooner at an end, than the popular orators revived domestic troubles, and raised another sedition, without any new cause of complaint or just grievance to proceed upon, but merely turning the very mischiefs that unavoidably ensued from their former contests into a pretext against the patricians. The greatest part of their arable land had been left unsown and without tillage, and the time of war allowing them no means or leisure to import provision from other countries, there was an extreme scarcity. The movers of the people then observing, that there was no corn to be bought, and that, if there had been, they had no money to buy it, began to calumniate the wealthy with false stories, and whisper it about, as if they, out of malice, had purposely contrived the famine. Meanwhile, there came an embassy from the Velitrani, proposing to deliver up their city to the Romans, and desiring they would send some new inhabitants to people it, as a late pestilential disease had swept away so many of the natives, that there was hardly a tenth part remaining of their whole community. This necessity of the Velitrani was considered by all more prudent people as most opportune in the present state of affairs; since the dearth made it needful to ease the city of its superfluous members, and they were in hope also, at the same time, to dissipate the gathering sedition by ridding themselves of the more violent and heated partisans, and discharging, so to say, the elements of disease and disorder in the state. The consuls, therefore, singled out such citizens to supply the desolation at Velitrae, and gave notice to others, that they should be ready to march against the Volscians, with the politic design of preventing intestine broils by employment abroad, and in the hope, that when rich as well as poor, plebeians and patricians, should be mingled again in the same army and the same camp, and engage in one common service for the public, it would mutually dispose them to reconciliation and friendship.

But Sicinnius and Brutus, the popular orators, interposed, crying out, that the consuls disguised the most cruel and barbarous action in the world under that mild and plausible name of a colony, and were simply precipitating so many poor citizens into a mere pit of destruction, bidding them settle down in a country where the air was charged with disease, and the ground covered with dead bodies, and expose themselves to the evil influence of a strange and angered deity. And then, as if it would not satisfy their hatred to destroy some by hunger, and offer others to the mercy of a plague, they must proceed to involve them also in a needless war of their own making, that no calamity might be wanting to complete the punishment of the citizens for refusing to submit to that of slavery to the rich.

By such addresses, the people were so possessed, that none of them would appear upon the consular summons to be enlisted for the war; and they showed entire aversion to the proposal for a new plantation; so that the senate was at a loss what to say or do. But Marcius, who began now to bear himself higher and to feel confidence in his past actions, conscious, too, of the admiration of the best and greatest men of Rome, openly took the lead in opposing the favorers of the people. The colony was dispatched to Velitrae, those that were chosen by lot being compelled to depart upon high penalties; and when they obstinately persisted in refusing to enroll themselves for the Volscian service, he mustered up his own clients, and as many others as could be wrought upon by persuasion, and with these made an inroad into the territories of the Antiates, where, finding a considerable quantity of corn, and collecting much booty, both of cattle and prisoners, he reserved nothing for himself in private, but returned safe to Rome, while those that ventured out with him were seen laden with pillage, and driving their prey before them. This sight filled those that had stayed at home with regret for their perverseness, with envy at their fortunate fellow-citizens, and with feelings of dislike to Marcius, and hostility to his growing reputation and power, which might probably be used against the popular interest.

Not long after he stood for the consulship; when, however, the people began to relent and incline to favor him, being sensible what a shame it would be to repulse and affront a man of his birth and merit, after he had done them so many signal services. It was usual for those who stood for offices among them to solicit and address themselves personally to the citizens, presenting themselves in the forum with the toga on alone, and no tunic under it; either to promote their supplications by the humility of their dress, or that such as had received wounds might more readily display those marks of their fortitude. Certainly, it was not out of suspicion of bribery and corruption that they required all such petitioners for their favor to appear ungirt and open, without any close garment; as it was much later, and many ages after this, that buying and selling crept in at their elections, and money became an ingredient in the public suffrages; proceeding thence to attempt their tribunals, and even attack their camps, till, by hiring the valiant, and enslaving iron to silver, it grew master of the state, and turned their commonwealth into a monarchy. For it was well and truly said that the first destroyer of the liberties of a people is he who first gave them bounties and largesses. At Rome the mischief seems to have stolen secretly in, and by little and little, not being at once discerned and taken notice of. It is not certainly known who the man was that did there first either bribe the citizens, or corrupt the courts; whereas, in Athens, Anytus, the son of Anthemion, is said to have been the first that gave money to the judges, when on his trial, toward the latter end of the Peloponnesian war, for letting the fort of Pylos fall into the hands of the enemy; in a period while the pure and golden race of men were still in possession of the Roman forum.

Marcius, therefore, as the fashion of candidates was showing the scars and gashes that were still visible on his body, from the many conflicts in which he had signalized himself during a service of seventeen years together they were, so to say, put out of countenance at this display of merit, and told one another that they ought in common modesty to create him consul. But when the day of election was now come, and Marcius appeared in the forum, with a pompous train of senators attending him; and the patricians all manifested greater concern, and seemed to be exerting greater efforts, than they had ever done before on the like occasion, the commons then fell off again from the kindness they had conceived for him, and in the place of their late benevolence, began to feel something of indignation and envy; passions assisted by the fear they entertained, that if a man of such aristocratic temper, and so influential among the patricians, should be invested with the power which that office would give him, he might employ it to deprive the people of all that liberty which was yet left them. In conclusion, they rejected Marcius. Two other names were announced, to the great mortification of the senators, who felt as if the indignity reflected rather upon themselves than on Marcius. He, for his part, could not bear the affront with any patience. He had always indulged his temper, and had regarded the proud and contentious element of human nature as a sort of nobleness and magnanimity; reason and discipline had not imbued him with that solidity and equanimity which enters so largely into the virtues of the statesman. He had never learned how essential it is for any one who undertakes public business, and desires to deal with mankind, to avoid above all things that self-will, which, as Plato says, belongs to the family of solitude; and to pursue, above all things, that capacity so generally ridiculed, of submission to ill treatment. Marcius, straightforward and direct, and possessed with the idea that to vanquish and overbear all apposition is the true part of bravery, and never imagining that it was the weakness and womanishness of his nature that broke out, so to say, in these ulcerations of anger, retired, full of fury and bitterness against the people. The young patricians, too, all that were proudest and most conscious of their noble birth, had always been devoted to his interest, and, adhering to him now, with a fidelity that did him no good, aggravated his resentment with the expression of their indignation and condolence. He had been their captain, and their willing instructor in the arts of war, when out upon expeditions, and their model in that true emulation and love of excellence which makes men extol, without envy or jealousy, each other's brave achievements.

In the midst of these distempers, a large quantity of corn reached Rome, a great part bought up in Italy, but an equal amount sent as a present from Syracuse, from Gelo, then reigning there. Many began now to hope well of their affairs, supposing the city, by this means, would be delivered at once, both of its want and discord. A council, therefore, being presently held, the people came flocking about the senate-house, eagerly awaiting the issue of that deliberation, expecting that the market prices would now be less cruel, and that what had come as a gift would be distributed as such. There were some within who so advised the senate; but Marcius, standing up, sharply inveighed against those who spoke in favor of the multitude, calling them flatterers of the rabble traitors to the nobility, and alleging, that, by such gratifications, they did but cherish those ill seeds of boldness and petulance that had been sown among the people, to their own prejudice, which they should have done well to observe and stifle at their first appearance, and not have suffered the plebeians to grow so strong, by granting them magistrates of such authority as the tribunes. They were, indeed, even now formidable to the state, since everything they desired was granted them; no constraint was put on their will; they refused obedience to the consuls, and, overthrowing all law and magistracy, gave the title of magistrate to their private factious leaders. "When things are come to such a pass, for us to sit here and decree largesses and bounties for them, like those Greeks where the populace is supreme and absolute, what would it be else," said he, "but to take their disobedience into pay, and maintain it for the common ruin of us all? They certainly cannot look upon these liberalities as a reward of public service, which they know they have so often deserted; nor yet of those secessions, by which they openly renounced their country; much less of the calumnies and slanders they have been always so ready to entertain against the senate; but will rather conclude that a bounty which seems to have no other visible cause or reason, must needs be the effect of our fear and flattery; and will, therefore, set no limit to their disobedience, nor ever cease from disturbances and sedition. Concession is mere madness; if we have any wisdom and resolution at all, we shall, on the contrary, never rest till we have recovered from them that tribunician power they have extorted from us; as being a plain subversion of the consulship, and a perpetual ground of separation in our city, that is no longer one, as heretofore, but has in this received such a wound and rupture, as is never likely to close and unite again, or suffer us to be of one mind, and to give over inflaming our distempers, and being a torment to each other."

Marcius, with much more to this purpose, succeeded, to an extraordinary degree, in inspiring the younger men with the same furious sentiments, and had almost all the wealthy on his side, who cried him up as the only person their city had, superior alike to force and flattery; some of the older men, however, opposed him, suspecting the consequences. As, indeed, there came no good of it; for the tribunes, who were present, perceiving how the proposal of Marcius took, ran out into the crowd with exclamations, calling on the plebeians to stand together, and come in to their assistance. The assembly met, and soon became tumultuous. The sum of what Marcius had spoken, having been reported to the people, excited them to such fury, that they were ready to break in upon the senate. The tribunes prevented this, by laying all the blame on Coriolanus, whom, therefore, they cited by their messengers to come before them, and defend himself. And when he contemptuously repulsed the officers who brought him the summons, they came themselves, with the Aediles, or overseers of the market, proposing to carry him away by force, and, accordingly, began to lay hold on his person. The patricians, however, coming to his rescue, not only thrust off the tribunes, but also beat the Aediles, that were their seconds in the quarrel; night, approaching, put an end to the contest. But, as soon as it was day, the consuls, observing the people to be highly exasperated, and that they ran from all quarters and gathered in the forum, were afraid for the whole city, so that, convening the senate afresh, they desired them to advise how they might best compose and pacify the incensed multitude by equitable language and indulgent decrees; since, if they wisely considered the state of things, they would find that it was no time to stand upon terms of honor, and a mere point of glory; such a critical conjuncture called for gentle methods, and for temperate and humane counsels. The majority, therefore, of the senators giving way, the consuls proceeded to pacify the people in the best manner they were able, answering gently to such imputations and charges as had been cast upon the senate, and using much tenderness and moderation in the admonitions and reproof they gave them. On the point of the price of provisions, they said, there should be no difference at all between them. When a great part of the commonalty was grown cool, and it appeared from their orderly and peaceful behavior that they had been very much appeased by what they had heard, the tribunes, standing up, declared, in the name of the people, that since the senate was pleased to act soberly and do them reason, they, likewise, should be ready to yield in all that was fair and equitable on their side; they must insist, however, that Marcius should give in his answer to the several charges as follows: first, could he deny that he instigated the senate to overthrow the government and annul the privileges of the people? and, in the next place, when called to account for it, did he not disobey their summons? and, lastly, by the blows and other public affronts to the Aediles, had he not done all he could to commence a civil war?

These articles were brought in against him, with a design either to humble Marcius, and show his submission if, contrary to his nature, he should now court and sue the people; or, if he should follow his natural disposition, which they rather expected from their judgment of his character, then that he might thus make the breach final between himself and the people.

He came, therefore, as it were, to make his apology, and clear himself; in which belief the people kept silence, and gave him a quiet hearing. But when, instead of the submissive and deprecatory language expected from him, he began to use not only an offensive kind of freedom, seeming rather to accuse than apologize, but, as well by the tone of his voice as the air of his countenance, displayed a security that was not far from disdain and contempt of them, the whole multitude then became angry, and gave evident signs of impatience and disgust; and Sicinnius, the most violent of the tribunes, after a little private conference with his colleagues, proceeded solemnly to pronounce before them all, that Marcius was condemned to die by the tribunes of the people, and bid the Aediles take him to the Tarpeian rock, and without delay throw him headlong from the precipice. When they, however, in compliance with the order, came to seize upon his body, many, even of the plebeian party, felt it to be a horrible and extravagant act; the patricians, meantime, wholly beside themselves with distress and horror, hurried up with cries to the rescue; and while some made actual use of their hands to hinder the arrest, and, surrounding Marcius, got him in among them, others, as in so great a tumult no good could be done by words, stretched out theirs, beseeching the multitude that they would not proceed to such furious extremities; and at length, the friends and acquaintance of the tribunes, wisely perceiving how impossible it would be to carry off Marcius to punishment without much bloodshed and slaughter of the nobility, persuaded them to forbear everything unusual and odious; not to dispatch him by any sudden violence, or without regular process, but refer the cause to the general suffrage of the people. Sicinnius then, after a little pause, turning to the patricians, demanded what their meaning was, thus forcibly to rescue Marcius out of the people's hands, as they were going to punish him; when it was replied by them, on the other side, and the question put, "Rather, how came it into your minds, and what is it you design, thus to drag one of the worthiest men of Rome, without trial, to a barbarous and illegal execution?" "Very well," said Sicinnius, "you shall have no ground in this respect for quarrel or complaint against the people. The people grant your request, and your partisan shall be tried. We appoint you, Marcius," directing his speech to him, "the third market-day ensuing, to appear and defend yourself, and to try if you can satisfy the Roman citizens of your innocence, who will then judge your case by vote." The patricians were content with such a truce and respite for that time, and gladly returned home, having for the present brought off Marcius in safety.

During the interval before the appointed time (for the Romans hold their sessions every ninth day, which from that cause are called nundinae in Latin), a war fell out with the Antiates, likely to be of some continuance, which gave them hope they might one way or other elude the judgment. The people, they presumed, would become tractable, and their indignation lessen and languish by degrees in so long a space, if occupation and war did not wholly put it out of their mind. But when, contrary to expectation, they made a speedy agreement with the people of Antium, and the army came back to Rome, the patricians were again in great perplexity, and had frequent meetings to consider how things might be arranged, without either abandoning Marcius, or yet giving occasion to the popular orators to create new disorders. Appius Claudius, whom they counted among the senators most averse to the popular interest, made a solemn declaration, and told them beforehand, that the senate would utterly destroy itself and betray the government, if they should once suffer the people to assume the authority of pronouncing sentence upon any of the patricians; but the oldest senators and most favorable to the people maintained, on the other side, that the people would not be so harsh and severe upon them, as some were pleased to imagine, but rather become more gentle and humane upon the concession of that power, since it was not contempt of the senate, but the impression of being contemned by it, which made them pretend to such a prerogative. Let that be once allowed them as a mark of respect and kind feeling, and the mere possession of this power of voting would at once dispossess them of their animosity.

When, therefore, Marcius saw that the senate was in pain and suspense upon his account, divided, as it were, betwixt their kindness for him and their apprehensions from the people, he desired to know of the tribunes what the crimes were they intended to charge him with, and what the heads of the indictment they would oblige him to plead to before the people; and being told by them that he was to be impeached for attempting usurpation, and that they would prove him guilty of designing to establish arbitrary government, stepping forth upon this, "Let me go then," he said, "to clear myself from that imputation before an assembly of them; I freely offer myself to any sort of trial, nor do I refuse any kind of punishment whatsoever; only," he continued, "let what you now mention be really made my accusation, and do not you play false with the senate." On their consenting to these terms, he came to his trial. But when the people met together, the tribunes, contrary to all former practice, extorted first, that votes should be taken, not by centuries, but tribes; a change, by which the indigent and factious rabble, that had no respect for honesty and justice, would be sure to carry it against those who were rich and well known, and accustomed to serve the state in war. In the next place, whereas they had engaged to prosecute Marcius upon no other head but that of tyranny, which could never be made out against him, they relinquished this plea, and urged instead, his language in the senate against an abatement of the price of corn, and for the overthrow of the tribunician power; adding further, as a new impeachment, the distribution that was made by him of the spoil and booty he had taken from the Antiates, when he overran their country, which he had divided among those that had followed him, whereas it ought rather to have been brought into the public treasury; which last accusation did, they say, more discompose Marcius than all the rest, as he had not anticipated he should ever be questioned on that subject, and, therefore, was less provided with any satisfactory answer to it on the sudden. And when, by way of excuse, he began to magnify the merits of those who had been partakers with him in the action, those that had stayed at home, being more numerous than the other, interrupted him with outcries. In conclusion, when they came to vote, a majority of three tribes condemned him; the penalty being perpetual banishment. The sentence of his condemnation being pronounced, the people went away with greater triumph and exultation than they had ever shown for any victory over enemies; while the senate was in grief and deep dejection, repenting now and vexed to the soul that they had not done and suffered all things rather than give way to the insolence of the people, and permit them to assume and abuse so great an authority. There was no need then to look at men's dresses, or other marks of distinction, to know one from another: any one who was glad was, beyond all doubt, a plebeian; any one who looked sorrowful, a patrician.

Marcius alone, himself, was neither stunned nor humiliated. In mien, carriage, and countenance, he bore the appearance of entire composure, and while all his friends were full of distress, seemed the only man that was not touched with his misfortune. Not that either reflection taught him, or gentleness of temper made it natural for him, to submit: he was wholly possessed, on the contrary, with a profound and deep-seated fury, which passes with many for no pain at all. And pain, it is true, transmuted, so to say, by its own fiery heat into anger, loses every appearance of depression and feebleness; the angry man makes a show of energy, as the man in a high fever does of natural heat, while, in fact, all this action of the soul is but mere diseased palpitation, distention, and inflammation. That such was his distempered state appeared presently plainly enough in his actions. On his return home, after saluting his mother and his wife, who were all in tears and full of loud lamentations, and exhorting them to moderate the sense they had of his calamity, he proceeded at once to the city gates, whither all the nobility came to attend him; and so, not so much as taking anything with him, or making any request to the company, he departed from them, having only three or four clients with him. He continued solitary for a few days in a place in the country, distracted with a variety of counsels, such as rage and indignation suggested to him; and proposing to himself no honorable or useful end, but only how he might best satisfy his revenge on the Romans, he resolved at length to raise up a heavy war against them from their nearest neighbors.

He determined, first to make trial of the Volscians, whom he knew to be still vigorous and flourishing, both in men and treasure, and he imagined their force and power was not so much abated, as their spite and auger increased, by the late overthrows they had received from the Romans.

There was a man of Antium, called Tullus Aufidius, who, for his wealth and bravery and the splendor of his family, had the respect and privilege of a king among the Volscians, but whom Marcius knew to have a particular hostility to himself, above all other Romans. Frequent menaces and challenges had passed in battle between them, and those exchanges of defiance to which their hot and eager emulation is apt to prompt young soldiers had added private animosity to their national feelings of opposition. Yet for all this, considering Tullus to have a certain generosity of temper, and knowing that no Volscian, so much as he, desired an occasion to requite upon the Romans the evils they had done, he did what much confirms the saying, that

Hard and unequal is with wrath the strife,
Which makes us buy its pleasure with our life.

Putting on such a dress as would make him appear to any whom he might meet most unlike what he really was, thus, like Ulysses, --

The town he entered of his mortal foes.

His arrival at Antium was about evening, and though several met him in the streets, yet he passed along without being known to any, and went directly to the house of Tullus, and, entering undiscovered, went up to the fire-hearth, and seated himself there without speaking a word, covering up his head. Those of the family could not but wonder, and yet they were afraid either to raise or question him, for there was a certain air of majesty both in his posture and silence, but they recounted to Tullus, being then at supper, the strangeness of this accident. He immediately rose from table and came in, and asked him who he was, and for what business he came thither; and then Marcius, unmuffling himself, and pausing awhile, "If," said he, "you cannot yet call me to mind, Tullus, or do not believe your eyes concerning me, I must of necessity be my own accuser. I am Caius Marcius, the author of so much mischief to the Volscians; of which, were I seeking to deny it, the surname of Coriolanus I now bear would be a sufficient evidence against me. The one recompense I received for all the hardships and perils I have gone through, was the title that proclaims my enmity to your nation, and this is the only thing which is still left me. Of all other advantages, I have been stripped and deprived by the envy and outrage of the Roman people, and the cowardice and treachery of the magistrates and those of my own order. I am driven out as an exile, and become an humble suppliant at your hearth, not so much for safety and protection (should I have come hither, had I been afraid to die?), as to seek vengeance against those that expelled me; which, methinks, I have already obtained, by putting myself into your hands. If, therefore, you have really a mind to attack your enemies, come then, make use of that affliction you see me in to assist the enterprise, and convert my personal infelicity into a common blessing to the Volscians; as, indeed, I am likely to be more serviceable in fighting for than against you, with the advantage, which I now possess, of knowing all the secrets of the enemy that I am attacking. But if you decline to make any further attempts, I am neither desirous to live myself, nor will it be well in you to preserve a person who has been your rival and adversary of old, and now, when he offers you his service, appears unprofitable and useless to you."

Tullus, on hearing this, was extremely rejoiced, and giving him his right hand, exclaimed, "Rise, Marcius, and be of good courage; it is a great happiness you bring to Antium, in the present you make us of yourself; expect everything that is good from the Volscians." He then proceeded to feast and entertain him with every display of kindness, and for several days after they were in close deliberation together on the prospects of a war.

While this design was forming, there were great troubles and commotions at Rome, from the animosity of the senators against the people, heightened just now by the late condemnation of Marcius. Besides that, their soothsayers and priests, and even private persons, reported signs and prodigies not to be neglected; one of which is stated to have occurred as follows: Titus Latinus, a man of ordinary condition, but of a quiet and virtuous character, free from all superstitious fancies, and yet more from vanity and exaggeration, had an apparition in his sleep, as if Jupiter came and bade him tell the senate, that it was with a bad and unacceptable dancer that they had headed his procession. Having beheld the vision, he said, he did not much attend to it at the first appearance; but after he had seen and slighted it a second and third time, he had lost a hopeful son, and was himself struck with palsy. He was brought into the senate on a litter to tell this, and the story goes, that he had no sooner delivered his message there, but he at once felt his strength return, and got upon his legs, and went home alone, without need of any support. The senators, in wonder and surprise, made a diligent search into the matter. That which his dream alluded to was this: some citizen had, for some heinous offense, given up a servant of his to the rest of his fellows, with charge to whip him first through the market, and then to kill him; and while they were executing this command, and scourging the wretch, who screwed and turned himself into all manner of shapes and unseemly motions, through the pain he was in, the solemn procession in honor of Jupiter chanced to follow at their heels. Several of the attendants on which were, indeed, scandalized at the sight, yet no one of them interfered, or acted further in the matter than merely to utter some common reproaches and execrations on a master who inflicted so cruel a punishment. For the Romans treated their slaves with great humanity in these times, when, working and laboring themselves, and living together among them, they naturally were more gentle and familiar with them. It was one of the severest punishments for a slave who had committed a fault, to have to take the piece of wood which supports the pole of a wagon, and carry it about through the neighborhood; a slave who had once undergone the shame of this, and been thus seen by the household and the neighbors, had no longer any trust or credit among them, and had the name of furcifer; furca being the Latin word for a prop, or support.

When, therefore, Latinus had related his dream, and the senators were considering who this disagreeable and ungainly dancer could be, some of the company, having been struck with the strangeness of the punishment, called to mind and mentioned the miserable slave who was lashed through the streets and afterward put to death. The priests, when consulted, confirmed the conjecture; the master was punished; and orders given for a new celebration of the procession and the spectacles in honor of the god. Numa, in other respects also a wise arranger of religious offices, would seem to have been especially judicious in his direction, with a view to the attentiveness of the people, that, when the magistrates or priests performed any divine worship, a herald should go before, and proclaim with a loud voice, Hoc age, Do this you are about, and so warn them to mind whatever sacred action they were engaged in, and not suffer any business or worldly avocation to disturb and interrupt it; most of the things which men do of this kind, being in a manner forced from them, and effected by constraint. It is usual with the Romans to recommence their sacrifices and processions and spectacles, not only upon such a cause as this, but for any slighter reason. If but one of the horses which drew the chariots called Tensae, upon which the images of their gods were placed, happened to fail and falter, or if the driver took hold of the reins with his left hand, they would decree that the whole operation should commence anew; and, in latter ages, one and the same sacrifice was performed thirty times over, because of the occurrence of some defect or mistake or accident in the service. Such was the Roman reverence and caution in religious matters.

Marcius and Tullus were now secretly discoursing of their project with the chief men of Antium, advising them to invade the Romans while they were at variance among themselves. And when shame appeared to hinder them from embracing the motion, as they had sworn to a truce and cessation of arms for the space of two years, the Romans themselves soon furnished them with a pretense, by making proclamation, out of some jealousy or slanderous report, in the midst of the spectacles, that all the Volscians who had come to see them should depart the city before sunset. Some affirm that this was a contrivance of Marcius, who sent a man privately to the consuls, falsely to accuse the Volscians of intending to fall upon the Romans during the games, and to set the city on fire. This public affront roused and inflamed their hostility to the Romans, and Tullus, perceiving it, made his advantage of it, aggravating the fact, and working on their indignation, till he persuaded them, at last, to dispatch ambassadors to Rome, requiring the Romans to restore that part of their country and those towns which they had taken from the Volscians in the late war. When the Romans heard the message, they indignantly replied, that the Volscians were the first that took up arms, but the Romans would be the last to lay them down. This answer being brought back, Tullus called a general assembly of the Volscians; and the vote passing for a war, he then proposed that they should call in Marcius, laying aside the remembrance of former grudges, and assuring themselves that the services they should now receive from him as a friend and associate, would abundantly outweigh any harm or damage he had done them when he was their enemy. Marcius was accordingly summoned, and having made his entrance, and spoken to the people, won their good opinion of his capacity, his skill, counsel, and boldness, not less by his present words than by his past actions. They joined him in commission with Tullus, to have full power as general of their forces in all that related to the war. And he, fearing lest the time that would be requisite to bring all the Volscians together in full preparation might be so long as to lose him the opportunity of action, left order with the chief persons and magistrates of the city to provide other things, while he himself, prevailing upon the most forward to assemble and march out with him as volunteers without staying to be enrolled, made a sudden inroad into the Roman confines, when nobody expected him, and possessed himself of so much booty, that the Volscians found they had more than they could either carry away or use in the camp. The abundance of provision which he gained, and the waste and havoc of the country which he made, were, however, of themselves and in his account, the smallest results of that invasion; the great mischief he intended, and his special object in all, was to increase at Rome the suspicions entertained of the patricians, and to make them upon worse terms with the people. With this view, while spoiling all the fields and destroying the property of other men, he took special care to preserve their farms and lands untouched, and would not allow his soldiers to ravage there, or seize upon anything which belonged to them. From hence their invectives and quarrels against one another broke out afresh, and rose to a greater height than ever; the senators reproaching those of the commonalty with their late injustice to Marcius; while the plebeians, on their side, did not hesitate to accuse them of having, out of spite and revenge, solicited him to this enterprise, and thus, when others were involved in the miseries of a war by their means, they sat like unconcerned spectators, as being furnished with a guardian and protector abroad of their wealth and fortunes, in the very person of the public enemy. After this incursion and exploit, which was of great advantage to the Volscians, as they learned by it to grow more hardy and to contemn their enemy, Marcius drew them off, and returned in safety.

But when the whole strength of the Volscians was brought together into the field, with great expedition and alacrity, it appeared so considerable a body, that they agreed to leave part in garrison, for the security of their towns, and with the other part to march against the Romans. Marcius now desired Tullus to choose which of the two charges would be most agreeable to him. Tullus answered, that since he knew Marcius to be equally valiant with himself, and far more fortunate, he would have him take the command of those that were going out to the war, while he made it his care to defend their cities at home, and provide all conveniences for the army abroad. Marcius thus reinforced, and much stronger than before, moved first towards the city called Circaeum, a Roman colony. He received its surrender, and did the inhabitants no injury; passing thence, he entered and laid waste the country of the Latins, where he expected the Romans would meet him, as the Latins were their confederates and allies, and had often sent to demand succors from them. The people, however, on their part, showing little inclination for the service, and the consuls themselves being unwilling to run the hazard of a battle, when the time of their office was almost ready to expire, they dismissed the Latin ambassadors without any effect; so that Marcius, finding no army to oppose him, marched up to their cities, and, having taken by force Toleria, Lavici, Peda, and Bola, all of which offered resistance, not only plundered their houses, but made a prey likewise of their persons. Meantime, he showed particular regard for all such as came over to his party, and, for fear they might sustain any damage against his will, encamped at the greatest distance he could, and wholly abstained from the lands of their property.

After, however, that he had made himself master of Bola, a town not above ten miles from Rome, where he found great treasure, and put almost all the adults to the sword; and when, on this, the other Volscians that were ordered to stay behind and protect their cities, hearing of his achievements and success, had not patience to remain any longer at home, but came hastening in their arms to Marcius, saying that he alone was their general and the sole commander they would own; with all this, his name and renown spread throughout all Italy, and universal wonder prevailed at the sudden and mighty revolution in the fortunes of two nations which the loss and the accession of a single man had effected.

All at Rome was in great disorder; they were utterly averse from fighting, and spent their whole time in cabals and disputes and reproaches against each other; until news was brought that the enemy had laid close siege to Lavinium, where were the images and sacred things of their tutelar gods, and from whence they derived the origin of their nation, that being the first city which Aeneas built in Italy. These tidings produced a change as universal as it was extraordinary in the thoughts inclinations of the people, but occasioned a yet stranger revulsion of feeling among the patricians. The people now were for repealing the sentence against Marcius, an calling him back into the city; whereas the senate, being assembled to preconsider the decree, opposed and finally rejected the proposal, either out of the mere humor of contradicting and withstanding the people in whatever they should desire, or because they were unwilling, perhaps, that he should owe his restoration to their kindness or having now conceived a displeasure against Marcius himself, who was bringing distress upon all alike, though he had not been ill treated by all, and was become, declared enemy to his whole country, though he knew well enough that the principal and all the better men condoled with him, and suffered in his injuries.

This resolution of theirs being made public, the people could proceed no further, having no authority to pass anything by suffrage, and enact it for a law, without a previous decree from the senate. When Marcius heard of this, he was more exasperated than ever, and, quitting the seige of Lavinium, marched furiously towards Rome, and encamped at a place called the Cluilian ditches, about five miles from the city. The nearness of his approach did, indeed, create much terror and disturbance, yet it also ended their dissensions for the present; as nobody now, whether consul or senator, durst any longer contradict the people in their design of recalling Marcius but, seeing their women running affrighted up and down the streets, and the old men at prayer in every temple with tears and supplications, and that, in short, there was a general absence among them both of courage and wisdom to provide for their own safety, they came at last to be all of one mind, that the people had been in the right to propose as they did a reconciliation with Marcius, and that the senate was guilty of a fatal error to begin a quarrel with him when it was a time to forget offenses, and they should have studied rather to appease him. It was, therefore, unanimously agreed by all parties, that ambassadors should be dispatched, offering him return to his country, and desiring he would free them from the terrors and distresses of the war. The persons sent by the senate with this message were chosen out of his kindred and acquaintance, who naturally expected a very kind reception at their first interview, upon the score of that relation and their old familiarity and friendship with him; in which, however, they were much mistaken. Being led through the enemy's camp, they found him sitting in state amidst the chief men of the Volscians, looking insupportably proud and arrogant. He bade them declare the cause of their coming, which they did in the most gentle and tender terms, and with a behavior suitable to their language. When they had made an end of speaking, he returned them a sharp answer, full of bitterness and angry resentment, as to what concerned himself, and the ill usage he had received from them; but as general of the Volscians, he demanded restitution of the cities and the lands which had been seized upon during the late war, and that the same rights and franchises should be granted them at Rome, which had been before accorded to the Latins; since there could be no assurance that a peace would be firm and lasting, without fair and just conditions on both sides. He allowed them thirty days to consider and resolve.

The ambassadors being departed, he withdrew his forces out of the Roman territory. This, those of the Volscians who had long envied his reputation, and could not endure to see the influence he had with the people laid hold of, as the first matter of complaint against him. Among them was also Tullus himself, not for any wrong done him personally by Marcius, but through the weakness incident to human nature. He could not help feeling mortified to find his own glory thus totally obscured, and himself overlooked and neglected now by the Volscians, who had so great an opinion of their new leader that he alone was all to them, while other captains, they thought, should be content with that share of power, which he might think fit to accord. From hence the first seeds of complaint and accusation were scattered about in secret, and the malcontents met and heightened each other's indignation, saying, that to retreat as he did was in effect to betray and deliver up, though not their cities and their arms, yet what was as bad, the critical times and opportunities for action, on which depend the preservation or the loss of everything else; since in less than thirty days' space, for which he had given a respite from the war, there might happen the greatest changes in the world. Yet Marcius spent not any part of the time idly, but attacked the confederates of the enemy ravaged their land, and took from them seven great and populous cities in that interval. The Romans, in the meanwhile, durst not venture out to their relief; but were utterly fearful, and showed no more disposition or capacity for action, than if their bodies had been struck with a palsy, and become destitute of sense and motion. But when the thirty days were expired, and Marcius appeared again with his whole army, they sent another embassy- to beseech him that he would moderate his displeasure, and would withdraw the Volscian army, and then make any proposals he thought best for both parties; the Romans would make no concessions to menaces, but if it were his opinion that the Volscians ought to have any favor shown them, upon laying down their arms they might obtain all they could in reason desire.

The reply of Marcius was, that he should make no answer to this as general of the Volscians, but, in the quality still of a Roman citizen, he would advise and exhort them, as the case stood, not to carry it so high, but think rather of just compliance, and return to him, before three days were at an end, with a ratification of his previous demands; otherwise, they must understand that they could not have any further freedom of passing through his camp upon idle errands.

When the ambassadors were come back, and had acquainted the senate with the answer, seeing the whole state now threatened as it were by a tempest, and the waves ready to overwhelm them, they were forced, as we say in extreme perils, to let down the sacred anchor. A decree was made, that the whole order of their priests, those who initiated in the mysteries or had the custody of them, and those who, according to the ancient practice of the country, divined from birds, should all and every one of them go in full procession to Marcius with their pontifical array, and the dress and habit which they respectively used in their several functions, and should urge him, as before, to withdraw his forces, and then treat with his countrymen in favor of the Volscians. He consented so far, indeed, as to give the deputation an admittance into his camp, but granted nothing at all, nor so much as expressed himself more mildly; but, without capitulating or receding, bade them once for all choose whether they would yield or fight, since the old terms were the only terms of peace. When this solemn application proved ineffectual, the priests, too, returning unsuccessful, they determined to sit still within the city, and keep watch about their walls, intending only to repulse the enemy, should he offer to attack them, and placing their hopes chiefly in time and in extraordinary accidents of fortune; as to themselves, they felt incapable of doing any thing for their own deliverance; mere confusion and terror and ill-boding reports possessed the whole city; till at last a thing happened not unlike what we so often find represented, without, however, being accepted as true by people in general, in Homer. On some great and unusual occasion we find him say: --

But him the blue-eyed goddess did inspire;

and elsewhere: --

But some immortal turned my mind away,
To think what others of the deed would say;

and again: --

Were 't his own thought or were 't a god's command.

People are apt, in such passages, to censure and disregard the poet, as if, by the introduction of mere impossibilities and idle fictions, he were denying the action of a man's own deliberate thought and free choice; which is not, in the least, the case in Homer's representation, where the ordinary, probable, and habitual conclusions that common reason leads to are continually ascribed to our own direct agency. He certainly says frequently enough: --

But I consulted with my own great soul;

or, as in another passage: --

He spoke. Achilles, with quick pain possessed,
Revolved two purposes in his strong breast;

and in a third: --

-- Yet never to her wishes won
The just mind of the brave Bellerophon.

But where the act is something out of the way and extraordinary, and seems in a manner to demand some impulse of divine possession and sudden inspiration to account for it here he does introduce divine agency, not to destroy, but to prompt the human will; not to create in us another agency, but offering images to stimulate our own; images that in no sort or kind make our action involuntary, but give occasion rather to spontaneous action, aided and sustained by feelings of confidence and hope. For either we must totally dismiss and exclude divine influences from every kind of causality and origination in what we do, or else what other way can we conceive in which divine aid and cooperation can act? Certainly we cannot suppose that the divine beings actually and literally turn our bodies and direct our hands and our feet this way or that, to do what is right: it is obvious that they must actuate the practical and elective element of our nature, by certain initial occasions, by images presented to the imagination, and thoughts suggested to the mind, such either as to excite it to, or avert and withhold it from, any particular course.

In the perplexity which I have described, the Roman women went, some to other temples, but the greater part, and the ladies of highest rank, to the altar of Jupiter Capitolinus. Among these suppliants was Valeria, sister to the great Poplicola, who did the Romans eminent service both in peace and war. Poplicola himself was now deceased, as is told in the history of his life; but Valeria lived still, and enjoyed great respect and honor at Rome, her life and conduct no way disparaging her birth. She, suddenly seized with the sort of instinct or emotion of mind which I have described, and happily lighting, not without divine guidance, on the right expedient, both rose herself, and bade the others rise, and went directly with them to the house of Volumnia, the mother of Marcius. And coming in and finding her sitting with her daughter-in-law, and with her little grandchildren on her lap, Valeria, then surrounded by her female companions, spoke in the name of them all:--

"We that now make our appearance, O Volumnia, and

you, Vergilia, are come as mere women to women, not by direction of the senate, or an order from the consuls, or the appointment of any other magistrate; but the divine being himself, as I conceive, moved to compassion by prayers, prompted us to visit you in a body, and request a thing on which our own and the common safety depends, and which, if you consent to it, will raise your glory above that of the daughters of the Sabines, who won over their fathers and their husbands from mortal enmity to peace and friendship. Arise and come with us to Marcius; join in our supplication, and bear for your country this true and just testimony on her behalf: that, notwithstanding the many mischiefs that have been done her, yet she has never outraged you, nor so much as thought of treating you ill, in all her resentment, but does now restore you safe into his hands, though there be small likelihood she should obtain from him any equitable terms."

The words of Valeria were seconded by the acclamations

of the other women, to which Volumnia made answer:--

"I and Vergilia, my countrywomen, have an equal share with you all in the common miseries, and we have the additional sorrow, which is wholly ours, that we have lost the merit and good fame of Marcius, and see his person confined, rather than protected, by the arms of the enemy. Yet I account this the greatest of all misfortunes, if indeed the affairs of Rome be sunk to so feeble a state as to have their last dependence upon us. For it is hardly imaginable he should have any consideration left for us, when he has no regard for the country which he was wont to prefer before his mother and wife and children. Make use, however, of our service; and lead us, if you please, to him; we are able, if nothing more, at least to spend our last breath in making suit to him for our country."

Having spoken thus, she took Vergilia by the hand, and the young children, and so accompanied them to the

Volscian camp. So lamentable a sight much affected the enemies themselves, who viewed them in respectful silence. Marcius was then sitting in his place, with his chief officers about him, and, seeing the party of women advance toward them, wondered what should be the matter; but perceiving at length that his mother was at the head of them, he would fain have hardened himself in his former inexorable temper, but, overcome by his feelings, and confounded at what he saw, he did not endure they should approach him sitting in state, but came down hastily to meet them, saluting his mother first, and embracing her a long time, and then his wife and children, sparing neither tears nor caresses, but suffering himself to be borne away and carried headlong, as it were, by the impetuous violence of his passion.

When he had satisfied himself, and observed that his mother Volumnia was desirous to say something, the Volscian council being first called in, he heard her to the following effect: "Our dress and our very persons, my son, might tell you, though we should say nothing ourselves, in how forlorn a condition we have lived at home since your banishment and absence from us; and now consider with yourself, whether we may not pass for the most unfortunate of all women, to have that sight, which should be the sweetest that we could see, converted, through I know not what fatality, to one of all others the most formidable and dreadful, -- Volumnia to behold her son, and Vergilia her husband, in arms against the walls of Rome. Even prayer itself, whence others gain comfort and relief in all manner of misfortunes, is that which most adds to our confusion and distress; since our best wishes are inconsistent with themselves, nor can we at the same time petition the gods for Rome's victory and your preservation, but what the worst of our enemies would imprecate as a curse, is the very object of our vows. Your wife and children are under the sad necessity, that they must either be deprived of you, or of their native soil. As for myself, I am resolved not to wait till war shall determine this alternative for me; but if I cannot prevail with you to prefer amity and concord to quarrel and hostility, and to be the benefactor to both parties, rather than the destroyer of one of them, be assured of this from me, and reckon steadfastly upon it, that you shall not be able to reach your country, unless you trample first upon the corpse of her that brought you into life. For it will be ill in me to wait and loiter in the world till the day come wherein I shall see a child of mine, either led in triumph by his own countrymen, or triumphing over them. Did I require you to save your country by ruining the Volscians, then, I confess, my son, the case would be hard for you to solve. It is base to bring destitution on our fellow- citizens; it is unjust to betray those who have placed their confidence in us. But, as it is, we do but desire a deliverance equally expedient for them and us; only more glorious and honorable on the Volscian side, who, as superior in arms, will be thought freely to bestow the two greatest of blessings, peace and friendship, even when they themselves receive the same. If we obtain these, the common thanks will be chiefly due to you as the principal cause; but if they be not granted, you alone must expect to bear the blame from both nations. The chance of all war is uncertain, yet thus much is certain in the present, that you, by conquering Rome, will only get the reputation of having undone your country; but if the Volscians happen to be defeated under your conduct, then the world will say, that, to satisfy a revengeful humor, you brought misery on your friends and patrons."

Marcius listened to his mother while she spoke, without answering her a word; and Volumnia, seeing him stand mute also for a long time after she had ceased, resumed: "O my son," said she, "what is the meaning of this silence? Is it a duty to postpone everything to a sense of injuries, and wrong to gratify a mother in a request like this? Is it the characteristic of a great man to remember wrongs that have been done him, and not the part of a great and good man to remember benefits such as those that children receive from parents, and to requite them with honor and respect? You, methinks, who are so relentless in the punishment of the ungrateful, should not be more careless than others to be grateful yourself. You have punished your country already; you have not yet paid your debt to me. Nature and religion, surely, unattended by any constraint, should have won your consent to petitions so worthy and so just as these; but if it must be so, I will even use my last resource." Having said this, she threw herself down at his feet, as did also his wife and children; upon which Marcius, crying out, "O mother! what is it you have done to me?" raised her up from the ground, and pressing her right hand with more than ordinary vehemence, "You have gained a victory," said he, "fortunate enough for the Romans, but destructive to your son; whom you, though none else, have defeated." After which, and a little private conference with his mother and his wife, he sent them back again to Rome, as they desired of him.

The next morning, he broke up his camp, and led the

Volscians homeward, variously affected with what he had done; some of them complaining of him and condemning his act, others, who were inclined to a peaceful conclusion, unfavorable to neither. A third party, while much disliking his proceedings, yet could not look upon Marcius as a treacherous person, but thought it pardonable in him to be thus shaken and driven to surrender at last, under such compulsion. None, however, opposed his commands; they all obediently followed him, though rather from admiration of his virtue, than any regard they now had to his authority. The Roman people, meantime, more effectually manifested how much fear and danger they had been in while the war lasted, by their deportment after they were freed from it. Those that guarded the walls had no sooner given notice that the Volscians were dislodged and drawn off, but they set open all their temples in a moment, and began to crown themselves with garlands and prepare for sacrifice, as they were wont to do upon tidings brought of any signal victory. But the joy and transport of the whole city was chiefly remarkable in the honors and marks of affection paid to the women, as well by the senate as the people in general; every one declaring that they were, beyond all question, the instruments of the public safety. And the senate having passed a decree that whatsoever they would ask in the way of any favor or honor should be allowed and done for them by the magistrates, they demanded simply that a temple might be erected to Female Fortune, the expense of which they offered to defray out of their own contributions, if the city would be at the cost of sacrifices, and other matters pertaining to the due honor of the gods, out of the common treasury. The senate, much commending their public spirit, caused the temple to be built and a statue set up in it at the public charge; they, however, made up a sum among themselves, for a second image of Fortune, which the Romans say uttered, as it was putting up, words to this effect, "Blessed of the gods, O women, is your gift."

These words they profess were repeated a second time, expecting our belief for what seems pretty nearly an impossibility. It may be possible enough, that statues may seem to sweat, and to run with tears, and to stand with certain dewy drops of a sanguine color; for timber and stones are frequently known to contract a kind of scurf and rottenness, productive of moisture; and various tints may form on the surfaces, both from within and from the action of the air outside; and by these signs it is not absurd to imagine that the deity may forewarn us. It may happen, also, that images and statues may sometimes make a noise not unlike that of a moan or groan, through a rupture or violent internal separation of the parts; but that an articulate voice, and such express words, and language so clear and exact and elaborate, should proceed from inanimate things, is, in my judgment, a thing utterly out of possibility. For it was never known that either the soul of man, or the deity himself, uttered vocal sounds and language, alone, without an organized body and members fitted for speech. But where history seems in a manner to force our assent by the concurrence of numerous and credible witnesses, we are to conclude that an impression distinct from sensation affects the imaginative part of our nature, and then carries away the judgment, so as to believe it to be a sensation: just as in sleep we fancy we see and hear, without really doing either. Persons, however, whose strong feelings of reverence to the deity, and tenderness for religion, will not allow them to deny or invalidate anything of this kind, have certainly a strong argument for their faith, in the wonderful and transcendent character of the divine power; which admits no manner of comparison with ours, either in its nature or its action, the modes or the strength of its operations. It is no contradiction to reason that it should do things that we cannot do, and effect what for us is impracticable: differing from us in all respects, in its acts yet more than in other points we may well believe it to be unlike us and remote from us. Knowledge of divine things for the most part, as Heraclitus says, is lost to us by incredulity.

When Marcius came back to Antium, Tullus, who thoroughly hated and greatly feared him, proceeded at once to contrive how he might immediately dispatch him; as, if he escaped now, he was never likely to give him such another advantage. Having, therefore, got together and suborned several partisans against him, he required Marcius to resign his charge, and give the Volscians all account of his administration. He, apprehending the danger of a private condition, while Tullus held the office of general and exercised the greatest power among his fellow- citizens, made answer, that he was ready to lay down his commission, whenever those from whose common authority he had received it, should think fit to recall it; and that in the meantime he was ready to give the Antiates satisfaction, as to all particulars of his conduct, if they were desirous of it.

An assembly was called, and popular speakers, as had been concerted, came forward to exasperate and incense the multitude; but when Marcius stood up to answer, the more unruly and tumultuous part of the people became quiet on a sudden, and out of reverence allowed him to speak without the least disturbance; while all the better people, and such as were satisfied with a peace, made it evident by their whole behavior, that they would give him a favorable hearing, and judge and pronounce according to equity.

Tullus, therefore, began to dread the issue of the defense he was going to make for himself; for he was an admirable speaker, and the former services he had done the Volscians had procured and still preserved for him greater kindness than could be outweighed by any blame for his late conduct. Indeed, the very accusation itself was a proof and testimony of the greatness of his merits, since people could never have complained or thought themselves wronged, because Rome was not brought into their power, but that by his means they had come so near to taking it. For these reasons, the conspirators judged it prudent not to make any further delays, nor to test the general feeling; but the boldest of their faction, crying out that they ought not to listen to a traitor, nor allow him still to retain office and play the tyrant among them, fell upon Marcius in a body, and slew him there, none of those that were present offering to defend him. But it quickly appeared that the action was in nowise approved by the majority of the Volscians, who hurried out of their several cities to show respect to his corpse; to which they gave honorable interment, adorning his sepulchre with arms and trophies, as the monument of a noble hero and a famous general. When the Romans heard tidings of his death, they gave no other signification either of honor or of anger towards him, but simply granted the request of the women, that they might put themselves into mourning and bewail him for ten months, as the usage was upon the loss of a father or a son or a brother; that being the period fixed for the longest lamentation by the laws of Numa Pompilius, as is more amply told in the account of him.

Marcius was no sooner deceased, but the Volscians felt the need of his assistance. They quarreled first with the Aequians, their confederates and their friends, about the appointment of the general of their joint forces, and carried their dispute to the length of bloodshed and slaughter; and were then defeated by the Romans in a pitched battle, where not only Tullus lost his life, but the principal flower of their whole army was cut in pieces; so that they were forced to submit and accept of peace upon very dishonorable terms, becoming subjects of Rome, and pledging themselves to submission.

Printed in Great Britain
by Amazon